# LULLING
# ROMAN



KENT

Michael Fulford

*The villa at Lullingstone is an outstanding example of a Roman villa, one of many stone houses – mainly farms – in the countryside of Roman Britain. They developed from the late first century* AD *and flourished until the end of the Roman administration of Britain at the beginning of the fifth century.*

*A number of such villas have been discovered in north Kent, near transport routes such as Watling Street or river valleys, including several here in the Darent valley. The wealth they display was probably based on supplying food to London and other Roman settlements. At Lullingstone, this wealth is shown in the fine mosaic floor which decorated the principal reception room of the late Roman villa. In addition, Lullingstone is particularly important for the evidence it provides for the development of Christianity in the fourth century.*

*Excavation of the site began in 1949, and continued under the direction of Lt Col G W Meates until 1961. Although much of what is visible today relates to the villa in the last hundred years or so of its life, sufficient evidence survives to reconstruct the development of the building, from the late first century until it was gutted by fire in the early fifth century, giving us a fascinating insight into Roman life in the British countryside.*

# CONTENTS



Lullingstone Roman Villa, Lullingstone Lane, Eynsford, Kent DA4 0JA. Tel no: 01322 863467

*Visit our website at www.english-heritage.org.uk*

*Published by English Heritage, Waterhouse Square, 138-142 Holborn, London EC1N 2ST*

*First published by English Heritage 2003, reprinted 2005, 2007*

*Edited by Susannah Charlton. Designed by Patricia Briggs. Picture research by Elaine Willis. Photography by Jonathan Bailey. Production by Elaine Pooke. Printed in England by Matthews the Printers Ltd. C45, 08/07, 04180, ISBN 1 85074 855 1*



*The plans of the villa were established by David Neal who was also responsible for the illustrations of the Christian plaster fragments on pp. 29–30. The editor would like to thank Jonathan Coad for his help, Miss Brenda Rose for permission to reproduce the photograph on page 20, and Mr S. Lomax for permission to use photographs from the collection of Mr J. Skeel.*

# TOUR OF THE VILLA

*The tour starts opposite the ticket desk, at the north of the site, and proceeds clockwise.*

From here you can look along the length of the villa and see the remains of the walls which constituted the rooms of this compactly built house, much as it was in the fourth century. The villa was developed in four phases over about three hundred and fifty years, starting in around AD 75. First came the living rooms in the

*Reconstruction drawing of the front of the villa, facing the river. The entrance to the site is now from the right*

PETER DUNN

*A view from the balcony, showing the suite of heated rooms on the north side, at the top of the picture*

centre of the plan, which were then extended, and a bath block added to the south. In the third phase the heated rooms immediately in front of you were built, and improvements made to the baths at the far end. Finally, the apsed dining room and mosaic in the centre were added, followed by changes reflecting the Christianity of the occupants.

## *Heated Rooms*

These rooms, heated by an underfloor heating system or hypocaust, represent a major modification of the villa on the north side dating from the late third century. Heat from a furnace situated under the current floor circulated beneath a floor supported originally on stacks of tiles (pilae), and up through flues set at intervals along the walls, which were thereby also heated. Hollow tiles of square section which made up the flues can be seen in the north and west walls of Room 3 and are best seen from upstairs. An arch in the wall separating Rooms 2 and 3 was originally beneath the floor and allowed the heat to pass from one room to the other.

The two flights of tiled steps in Room 3 originally led down to the adjacent cellar. At the bottom the tiled door jamb shows where there was once a door into the cellar.

The advantage of heating rooms in this way was that one furnace could be used as a single source of heat for several rooms; the flues in the walls drawing the hot air under the floors and up the walls. Rooms heated in this way would have served as the principal living and sleeping quarters of the villa at the time. Alternative approaches were to heat individual rooms, using braziers or fireplaces similar to those used in modern times. As with any form of heating it is likely that frequency of use was regulated by the cost; fires were probably only lit regularly to combat the cold and damp of the winter months. When abandoned about the middle of the fourth century these heated rooms were not similarly replaced elsewhere in the villa.

In the fourth century the hypocaust was filled and a timber floor constructed, of which the slots for the joists are visible at the top of the far walls separating the cellar from

# ❖ THE EXCAVATOR ❖

Geoffrey Meates had retired from the army in 1945 having served with distinction in India and, during the Second World War, first in the British Expeditionary Force to France evacuated from Dunkirk in 1940, and then as Commanding Officer of the anti-aircraft regiment defending Malta during the siege. After the war, living locally, and as a newcomer to archaeology, he joined the Darenth Valley Archaeological Group which was surveying Roman settlement in the valley. He took over sole direction of the excavation of Lullingstone in 1953, and worked there until 1961. Meates then went on with others to excavate the ruined church of Stone-next-Faversham, Kent in 1967, proving that the church had been built on the foundations of a Roman mausoleum. Col. Meates was a member of the Kent Archaeological Society from 1947, and elected Fellow of the Society of Antiquaries in 1950.

*Geoffrey Meates overseeing the cleaning of the mosaics during the excavation of Lullingstone*

Rooms 1 and 2. Later in the fourth century Room 3 became an ante-room to the house church or private chapel next door. Fragments were recovered during the excavation of a Christian Chi-Rho monogram in red within a wreath of leaves and buds which had been painted on the south wall.

*Follow the walkway round the corner to the next room, on the east of the villa.*

## *The Deep Room*

The deep room is one of the most interesting rooms of the villa. For much, if not all of its life it was used as a cult room. In the fourth century a house church occupied the room directly above. It dates back to when the house was first constructed and, although undergoing several major changes, it remained in use for the rest of the life of the villa. As seen today it appears to have no entrance, but remains of steps are clearly visible in the far right (north-west) corner (on the other side of the blocked doorway from Room 3). Another entrance, also blocked up, but represented by traces of a wooden staircase, led down from the verandah to the left (south). What is particularly exciting about this room is that its depth helped to preserve its contents at the time of the destruction and collapse of the room above. These give us important insights into the way it was used.

PETER DUNN

*This reconstruction illustration shows the Christian House Church above the Cult Room. The square well and painted niche can still be seen in this room*

## *The Cult Room*

The excavator argued that this space was originally used for storage, but in the second century it was clearly devoted to a pagan cult. It could be approached from three directions, which led to one entrance in the north-west where the steps survive. The original entrance from the south was then blocked and the round-headed niche you can see on the left constructed in its place with a small, square well in front of it. In the niche can be seen the remains of a painted scene of three water nymphs, suggesting the worship of a water cult. The remaining walls were also decorated with painted plaster, some of which was still on the walls at the time of the excavation. Beside the stairs this showed a yellow palm-tree motif with red fruit, and remains of a similar scheme were found in the adjacent room pre-dating the heated rooms.

Two pots dating from the late second century were found placed separately in shallow pits at the west end of the cellar. One of the pots was a small beaker made in the Rhineland and painted with the word SVAVIS meaning sweet; the other was a local cooking pot. They are on display upstairs.

Major changes took place after the late third century, when the entrance from the north was blocked. The niche was filled in with mortared flints, severely damaging the painted plaster, and the room was redecorated with white plaster painted with red bands. Four piers were built against the north and south walls. It is not clear how the room was now entered,

J SKEEL

*A watercolour of two of the nymphs in the Cult Room niche. Note the water flowing from the breasts of one nymph, and the overturned vessel on the left*

J SKEEL

*A beaker, inscribed SVAVIS, meaning sweet, was found in the cellar*

# ❖ ROMAN PAGAN CULTS ❖

There is a wealth of evidence from Roman Britain representing the rich variety of empire-wide religions and of more local cults which helped structure everyday life. There was the worship of Roman gods like Jupiter, Juno and Minerva as well as living and dead emperors and the spirit of the imperial family. These helped impose a Roman identity on a diverse and geographically extensive empire. Not surprisingly, much of the evidence for this comes from the military areas of Britain where it was vital to retain the loyalty of the army. The army also included worshippers of eastern 'mystery' cults, such as that of Mithras from Persia, whose victory over death offered a similar possibility to his devotees.

Locally there were cults whose origins lay in the pre-Roman past, many of which were expressed in sculpture and dedications for the first time in Roman Britain. They might be specific to a locality, such as a spring or river, like the water cult in the deep room at Lullingstone. More famously, at Bath the native goddess Sulis, paired with Roman Minerva, presided over the hot springs, while at the fort at Carrawburgh on Hadrian's Wall the Celtic deity Coventina was associated with a well to which many offerings were made. It is rare in Britain to find evidence of worship in Classical-style temples. To date, we have only found two, one dedicated to Emperor Claudius at Colchester, and the other to Sulis Minerva in Bath. The usual Romano-Celtic temple consisted of a small rectangular central shrine surrounded by a rectangular walkway, not dissimilar in plan and scale to the Lullingstone mausoleum. As at Lullingstone, there is much evidence for the continuity of pagan cults, as represented by Romano-Celtic temples alongside Christian worship in the fourth century.

*Wall-painting of three water nymphs in the Deep Room. The head of the central nymph, with her long dark hair and brown eyes, is still well preserved.*

perhaps through a trap-door from the room above. This seems to coincide with a change in the cult, when the worship of the spirits of ancestors and household gods may have replaced the water cult. On the steps were placed two marble busts of bearded men in Roman dress (modern replicas can now be seen upstairs; the originals are in the British Museum).

Two further complete cooking pots were found inserted into a new clay floor of the room and the well continued to serve as a water supply. To its west lying on the floor were five specialised pottery vessels, distinguished by the grits pressed into their internal surfaces (*mortaria*) and normally used in the preparation of food, as well as a pottery flagon. By the bottom step was found a roughly shaped and weathered limestone block whose carving was worn, but which the excavator believed had a feline or leonine face carved on its front.

The busts are carved from Greek Pentelic marble and both are dated to the second or third quarter of the second century. They are East Mediterranean in style and designed to stand in niches. One, possibly the earlier of the two, wears a military-style fringed cloak clasped by a circular brooch, while the other is portrayed in a civilian toga. There is some resemblance between the two faces and they may have been related.

SOCIETY OF ANTIQUARIES

*The two marble busts where they were found during excavation*

*Cellar steps, which were blocked at the bottom by the inserted hypocaust wall*

## Christian House Church

*Painted wall-plaster head of the second figure from the west wall, as reconstructed below*

*This image of six early Christians praying is a modern reconstruction of the wall painting from the west wall of the house church, or chapel. It has been painstakingly pieced together from the fragments of painted plaster which had fallen into the cult room below*

The most exciting discovery came at an earlier stage of the excavation with the removal of the fill of the cellar, which consisted of all the debris from the collapse into it of the room above. It had been decorated with painted wall plaster, the fragments of which have been pieced together to show six standing figures, about one-third life size, separated from each other by painted columns and with their arms outstretched in the attitude of early Christian prayer. They wear long-sleeved tunics with beaded sashes down the centre and across the tunic; one of the figures appears to have a curtain behind him. This painting probably came from the west wall, while from the south wall came the fragments of a second, large Chi-Rho monogram, set in a wreath and flanked by painted columns, and similar to that found in the adjacent Room 3. The reconstructed plaster can be seen in the British Museum. These discoveries remain among the most significant evidence for early Christianity in Britain.

J SKEEL

*Continue along the east side of the villa*

BRITISH MUSEUM

## *East Verandah*

The verandah ran along the east side of the audience chamber and dining room and linked the 'wing rooms' to the north and south. The east wall was probably open with dwarf columns giving a fine view across the river. Its floor level was about 1.5m (4 feet) above the ground level outside. At the north end can be seen traces of the early staircase leading down to the cellar room and the remains of a tiled drain leading from the corner of the audience chamber. The east façade of the villa provided the most impressive elevation of the building, and may have been the main entrance.

## *South Wing*

No floors survive in this room which was probably a living room, matching that over the deep room before it was converted to the House Church.

## *Unidentified Room*

There was no evidence to determine the function of this room, but some remarkable finds were made here. In the fourth century a pit was cut into the floor, into which was placed a large storage jar made in the Alice Holt potteries (Surrey). This vessel is in its original position. Around it were packed a number of objects including very rare items such as a bronze lion fitting, a circular padlock and chain and a finely decorated glass bowl, as well as other glass drinking and pottery vessels and several coins dated 330-50. It is far from clear whether the large jar was used to store liquid, other materials or, as the excavator suggested, used as a latrine. However, the selection and deposition of items has a distinctly votive character.

Opposite, in a shallow burial cut through the floor were the remains of an infant. Associated with it were some fourth century coins, a handful of carbonised wheat and a fragment of figured bronze. Deeper excavation on the west side of the room revealed another remarkable find: an earlier pit of late first or early second century which contained four large ingots and a circular casting of copper, probably of British origin, alloyed with about forty per cent of lead. Such a high ratio of lead to copper is extremely unusual for bronze, and if worked would have been liable to tearing.

*Walk along to the corner*

*View from the balcony showing the East Verandah beyond the mosaics, the South Wing, and the baths at the far end. Note the large jar in the corner of the unidentified room*

*A cylindrical glass bottle with elegant dolphin handles found in 33 fragments*

## *Baths*

The baths were constructed towards the end of the second century at a lower level than the main house, reached by a flight of stairs connecting with the southern end of the west corridor. The building shows evidence of a complex history but its essential components are three rooms: a hot room or *caldarium*, a place where bathers could sweat located directly next to the furnace and fuel store, a room of tepid heat or *tepidarium*, and a cold room without a hypocaust known as a *frigidarium*. The room north of and adjacent to the furnace and *caldarium* was possibly a *laconicum*, a hot dry room. The source of water was probably a tank at the east end.

Bathing was an important activity for those who assumed a Romanised lifestyle and the baths at Lullingstone were a miniature of the larger city baths found throughout the Roman Empire. Here not only the family would meet to get clean, but also visitors, perhaps from neighbouring estates, might come to discuss business and politics. Turkish baths, where bathers sweat out the dirt rather than wash it off, represent the modern counterpart. Bathing was a relatively lengthy process; bathers would progress from warm room (*tepidarium*) to hot (*caldarium*) and then revisit the warm room or plunge directly into a cold bath (*frigidarium*). Given the effort of filling the baths with clean water (eye infections, probably the result of bathing in dirty water, were common in the Roman world) and of generating the heat, it is likely that the baths were used periodically, rather than every day, and, when prepared, by the whole household.

The floors of the heated rooms were supported on small stacks of tiles (*pilae*); as with the heated rooms to the north heat passed under the raised floors and up the walls through flues or small chimneys. These basic facilities also included hot and cold plunge baths. Close to the furnace, and distinguished by its jacketing of flue-tiles, was a hot bath with its drain leading through the south wall. A larger cold bath appears to have replaced the original *frigidarium*. It was originally decorated with an aquatic scene; fragments of wall plaster painted with fish were recovered here. In the sides of a pit, which cuts the floor, you can see how the first floor was covered by a later one. Also notice the extensive use of a pink cement

*The heated rooms of the bath suite. Note the stacks of tiles which would have supported the floor. The furnace is in the foreground, and the cold bath at the far end*

known as *opus signinum*, its colour derived from crushed tile, often old roofing tiles. The Romans discovered that by mixing crushed tile or other ceramics with lime mortar and other aggregates, they could produce a cement which was impermeable to water when set, and it was used widely throughout the Empire.

*Continue round to the south side.*

## *Well*

Water for the baths may originally have been supplied from this well on the south side of the villa. It was lined with flints resting on an oak frame and is cut into the chalk to a depth of 2.75m (9 feet). How the water was raised is unclear, but a bucket hoop was found at the bottom. It seems to have been abandoned at the end of the second or beginning of the third century and water for the baths may have been supplied by tapping the river from higher up the valley. In the waterlogged silts at the base of the well were many fragments of pine cone from the Stone Pine *Pinus pinea*. This was often burnt on altars to give off a pungent aroma.

## *Fuel Store*

This room, located next to the furnace identified by its scorched walls, was a store for the wood fuel used to stoke the fire. Although we do not know how frequently the baths were in operation, intensive use of the furnace, indicated by evidence of wear and repairs to its sides and to the floor supports, suggests that the baths were well used. Fuel consumption to heat the baths would have been at the rate of over 50 kg of wood per hour. A hot water tank or *testudo* would have been placed over the furnace. It was probably made of bronze, supported on massive forged iron beams, in an arrangement similar to that found in the Suburban Baths in Herculaneum, Italy.

*For the best view, walk upstairs to the gallery. Alternatively, continue along the west of the villa at ground level.*

## *West corridor*

This once ran along the full length of the villa and probably acted as the main service passage for the villa staff, giving access to an adjacent kitchen block. In the fourth century it was cut by the construction of the dining room, and linked to the east side of the villa by a narrow passage.

*View of the site from the South, with the baths in the foreground*

*A fine Cornelian intaglio depicting Victory. Superbly carved it is only 24mm (an inch) long. It was found just outside the west wall of the villa*

*The magnificent mosaics that adorned the main reception rooms of the house. They depict mythological scenes, with roundels of the seasons, and elaborate geometric borders*

## Dining Room and Audience Chamber

From the centre you get a good overview of the plan of the villa. To the left lie the suite of heated rooms, with their tiled heating ducts visible in the wall, and beside them the Deep Room with its square well. To the right of the main rooms can be seen further living rooms and, at a lower level on the far right, the heated baths.

In front of you lies one of the most spectacular finds of the villa: the magnificent pair of mosaics, reliably dated by coins to the mid-fourth century, on the floor of the main dining (*triclinium*) and reception room. These represent the most important rooms of the house. The nearer, apsidal space was for dining. The mosaic is oriented so that diners, reclining on couches laid on the semi-circular expanse of red tiled floor around it, could enjoy the scene and read the quotation of Latin poetry above it. They would also have been able to look out through the east verandah to the river and land on the other side of the valley, which perhaps formed part of the villa's estate.

The mosaics were laid when the original dining room (*triclinium*) was extended in the mid-fourth century by adding the semi-circular apse.

## ❖ MOSAIC TECHNIQUES ❖

Mosaics are made up of patterns of small cubes of durable, coloured material, usually stone, but also ceramic and glass. It seems that this form of floor decoration originated in the Greek world between the fourth and the second century BC. In Roman Britain the earliest floors date from the late first century AD. Making mosaics was a highly skilled task and it is likely that demand was met by specialised workshops, of which a number have been suggested for Roman Britain on the basis of common elements of design. It is likely that complex, figured compositions, like these here at Lullingstone, were made up on site, but using pattern books to establish the design which would have been marked out beforehand on the working surface. The materials used at Lullingstone are tile (where the dark blue is derived from the core of tiles otherwise fired red on the outside), chalk (white) and Wealden sandstone ranging in colour from purple to near black. It is possible that some of the fine detail of the hair of Europa and of the Cupids is made up from imported coloured marbles.

*This depiction of Winter shows how the image is made up from tiny coloured tesserae*

IVSTIVSAEOLIASISSETADVSQVEDOMOS

*These decorative motifs in the mosaic include hearts among the geometric designs*

The mosaics show two mythological scenes, with roundels showing the seasons. The one showing Summer was destroyed by an eighteenth-century post-hole. Separating the two mythical scenes is a geometric design based on four rows of motifs in squares. The whole design is framed with other geometric patterns and a Greek key design, while coarse red tesserae cover the rest of the floor.

## Possible Bedroom and Kitchen

Adjacent to the west corridor was a possible bedroom. Originally it was larger, its floor being carried across part of the cellar. Two small hoards, one of eighteen, the other of four bronze coins dating to the first half of the of fourth century coins were found dug into shallow pits in the floor close to the west wall.

In the north-west corner may once have been a kitchen. A large pit was found dug into the north-west corner containing several coins of the mid-fourth century. Three roughly made cooking pots, at least two iron knives and animal bones, including parts of skulls were found here. By the late fourth century this room had become the vestibule to the House Church with an entrance to the outside in its north wall, and to Heated Room 3 in its east wall.

*Of the four other structures near the main house which have been excavated, only the circular building remains visible. To see it, go outside and walk up the path on the left. The others – including a granary and mausoleum – are described in the history section* *(see page 20).*

## Circular Building

Lt Col Meates believed that the second century circular building found about 25 metres north-west of the villa was a shrine. Remains of mortared flint foundations, perhaps to support a timber rather than a masonry superstructure, were found. The interior was partly surfaced with coarse tile tesserae and there were fragments of red and white-painted wall plaster. No artefacts were found which could help to interpret its use and circular domestic buildings have since been found in Roman Britain. However, it is close to the temple mausoleum and may have had a similar purpose.

*The surviving remains of the circular building, showing an excavated section beneath the floor. Part of the edge of the building has been lost due to erosion*

# THE HISTORY OF LULLINGSTONE VILLA

## Roman Britain

The conquest of Roman Britain was begun by the Emperor Claudius in AD 43 and the south-east including Kent was pacified within a very few years. Although London was destroyed in AD 60 by the rebellion of Boudicca, the leader of the tribe of the Iceni (East Anglia), there is no evidence of further destruction to the south-east. The province undoubtedly experienced some difficult times, such as when the governor, Clodius Albinus, tried to seize control of the empire (AD 193-7), or when it was in the hands of the usurper emperors Carausius and Allectus (AD 287-96), but for the most part life in the south of the island was peaceful. This enabled town life to be nurtured and sustained with the population engaged, for the most part, in farming centred on villages or villas like Lullingstone. Life became more difficult in the second half of the fourth century as Rome found it harder to retain control of all its territories and, eventually, by 409-10 it finally lost its authority over Britain.

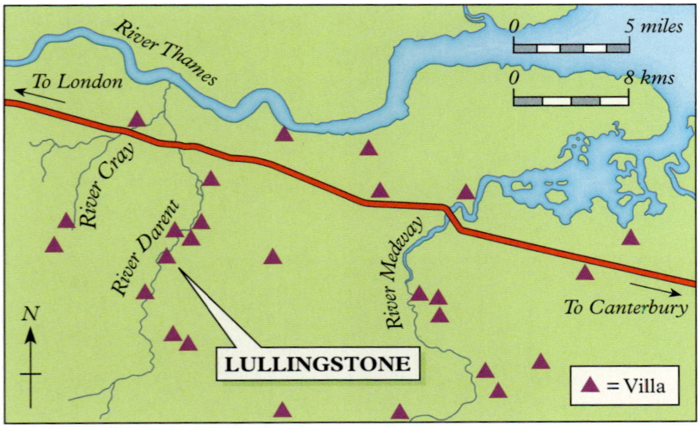


*Map showing the Roman villas that clustered in this area, near transport routes to the markets in London*

## Roman Villas of the Darent Valley

Lullingstone is one of a number of villas that have been discovered in north Kent. They tend to be located close either to Watling Street, the

*Brown-slipped pottery flagon manufactured near Oxford; associated with the burials in the mausoleum about AD 300*

*The granary under excavation*

Roman road running south-east from London to Rochester, Canterbury and the port at Richborough, or to the valleys of north-flowing rivers such as the Medway and the Cray. In between these rivers, Lullingstone is one of several comparable villa sites ranged evenly along the length of the Darent valley, about twenty miles from the centre of London. The main residential building is situated just above the flood-plain, and at least one of the outbuildings, the granary, is located within twenty metres of the river. Lullingstone was situated in the administrative, or tribal canton of the Cantiaci of which the principal town was Canterbury (*Durovernum Cantiacorum*). Nearer at hand was the small town of Rochester (*Durobrivae*) on the River Medway.

The wealth displayed by the villas of the Darent valley is probably related to their ability to take advantage of markets for food and other agricultural products in London and further afield. While food is difficult to track archaeologically, the distribution of more durable finds of south-east British origin can be traced. Types of pottery which were made in north Kent in the second and third century AD have been found in settlements up the east coast of England, as far as the northern frontiers of the Roman province on the Antonine Wall and Hadrian's Wall, as well as more locally in London. It might reasonably be inferred from this evidence that some at least of the produce of Lullingstone and its neighbours went further afield to feed the garrisons of the northern frontier. Given that little work has been done to establish the agricultural role of these villas and the possible extent of their dependent estates, it is also possible that some of them were the country houses of magnates who had made their fortune elsewhere.

What is known about the villa complex at Lullingstone is incomplete. If it were not for the discovery of the granary there would be no evidence that the villa was part of a working farm. On the basis of the tentative calculations to estimate storage capacity it has been estimated that the arable land at Lullingstone might approximate between about 600 and 900 acres. We ought also to allow pasture for stock, invaluable for manuring the land, and, possibly, for orchards, vineyards and woodland, which might point to a total size of between about 1100 and 1700 acres (between about 500 and 800 hectares). The excavation produced plentiful evidence of cattle, sheep and pig, as well as of fowl. It is particularly tempting to reconstruct an orchard as part of the estate on the basis of the fruit stones recovered from the pit outside the kitchens. These included sloe, bird cherry, bullace and cherry plum. Vines were certainly cultivated in Roman Britain and could have been grown at Lullingstone, although there is no direct evidence for this.

To work such an estate would have required a large labour force of about twenty to thirty people, probably supplemented by casual labour at harvest time, many more than might be accommodated in the villa house which would have probably been restricted to the family and some servants. It is highly likely that more buildings remain to be discovered. If the estate extended across the valley like the medieval parish, it is possible that buildings are to be found there.

We do not know who owned the villa, or whether ownership changed with time. Throughout its history the villa shows evidence of wealth, represented by the quality of the decoration and some of the finds, of education, reflected by the choice of mythological scenes for the mosaics and the Latin verse couplet, and of a religious sensitivity, reflected in the remarkable diversity and sophistication of cult and religion. Altogether it is hard to find a close parallel to the Lullingstone household on the basis of the material finds. Equally tantalising are the two marble busts which, if they are family portraits, suggest a link with the eastern empire. Does this imply that members of the family served in the army or the imperial service in the east in a senior capacity? Or does it signify a change of ownership in the third century? On the whole, the evidence for continuity of cult, albeit on a changing basis, but in itself remarkable, implies continuity of ownership. Perhaps at Lullingstone we have the ancestral home of a Romano-British family which, in the second century, had a distinguished record of imperial service.

If a villa represents the more comfortable end of living in Roman Britain, there are some reminders of a harsher life. The excavation produced the remains of three infants which had died at birth or in early infancy, and two adults buried in the mausoleum at the beginning of the fourth century were in their early twenties.

*The marble bust of a distinguished Roman of about 50, wearing semi-military dress. The original is in the British Museum*

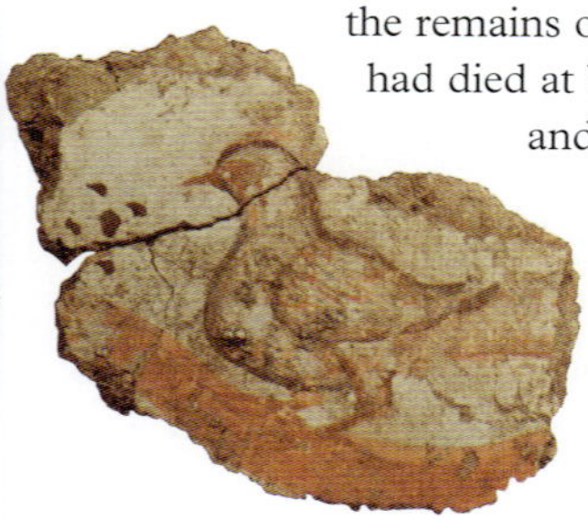

*Painted wall-plaster showing a bird standing on orange ribbon which ties the wreath around the Chi-Rho monogram from the south wall of the House Church*

## HISTORY OF DISCOVERY AND EXCAVATION

The existence of a Roman site at Lullingstone was known back in the early nineteenth century, but only relocated in 1939, close to the outbreak of the Second World War. Excavation did not commence until 1949, under the direction, first of the Darenth Valley Archaeological Group and, subsequently, solely by Lt Col G W Meates (1900-85). Work continued under his direction until 1961. In recognition of the importance of the remains, the site was taken into the Guardianship of the state in 1958 and, following the construction of a cover building, was opened to the public in 1963.

The visible remains only represent a part of what was excavated. Between the villa house and the river was a granary building. This large rectangular building, measuring some 24 by 10 m, is located beneath and

## ❖ HOW LULLINGSTONE WAS EXCAVATED ❖

Before commencing an excavation it is important to understand the extent of the remains. Whereas now we might investigate the extent and layout of a site using non-destructive geophysical techniques of survey, in the case of Lullingstone a long iron probe was used. The area was then divided by a grid system into a series of squares and rectangles which were excavated, and the contents recorded, from the turf down to the underlying occupation levels. This system provided an accurate three-dimensional record, not only of what was found, but also of the build-up of deposits which had preserved the history of the occupation of the site. Eventually the baulks between each square were themselves excavated to reveal the entirety of the plan of the villa and its associated buildings. Such an approach to excavation, where much is initially obscured beneath the baulks of unexcavated ground between the squares, has now been overtaken by a technique which examines larger areas where, if possible, the entirety of the archaeological deposit is carefully excavated and recorded, layer by layer.

*This photograph of volunteer Miss Brenda Rose at work clearly shows how sections of the site were excavated in a grid pattern, leaving baulks of earth in between*

beside the slip road into the car park. It was built in the early fourth century. The presence within it of a distinctive series of stacks of mortared flint to support a timber floor identify its main use as a granary. Air entered through small arches located in the gable ends and circulated beneath the floor to prevent the decay of grain stored above. On the short axis of the building were three rectangular compartments which probably had solid floors to act as loading bays or threshing floors. The raised timber floor was largely abandoned late in the fourth century, when it is suggested that the building may have served as a barn. Quantities of broken eggshells suggest that the room on the south side may have been used for keeping chickens.

This is one of the largest granaries associated with a villa in Roman Britain and it clearly indicates that corn, probably mainly wheat and barley, was a major crop from the villa's estate in the fourth century. Assuming that the sacks of corn were stacked two high, the granary might have stored about 3,500 bushels (about 28,000 gallons or 185,000 litres).

On the higher ground behind the villa to the west the excavators found another detached rectangular building, possibly representing the kitchen. Measuring some nine by six metres (thirty by twenty feet), it was supported on substantial wooden posts, and lay terraced into the hillside some three metres to the west of the villa. In one corner, perhaps buried at the time of construction in the first half of the second century, were the remains of an infant. The interpretation of it as a kitchen derives from the remains of two ovens at the west end of the building and the trampled remains of ash, burnt pottery vessels and broken bird bones.

Two large pits were found immediately outside to the west. One of these contained at its base a very large and concentrated deposit of seeds, pips and fruit stones, which lay above a sheet of leather and a large number of leather sandals pressed into a clay lining. This led Meates to believe that the building was

*Housewives, schoolboys, students and other volunteers helped to excavate Lullingstone. Lt Col Meates is in the far left corner of the picture*

*The body of a young man in a lead sarcophagus was found in the mausoleum behind the villa*

*The scallop-shell patterns on the end of the coffin*

converted into a tannery at the end of the second century. However, it is more likely that the pits served as latrines, which are often found close to kitchens in the Roman world.

Like the circular building, the only one of these buildings to be visible today, the temple mausoleum lay above and to the west of the villa house. Its plan, which comprises a central square *cella* surrounded by an ambulatory, is similar to that of Romano-Celtic temples. The building was an elaborate structure, the *cella* decorated with painted plaster and probably with a vaulted roof. Set into its floor was a timber-lined pit which contained a lead coffin decorated with embossed scallop shells (on display near the start of the tour) and evidence that a second coffin had been removed by grave robbers, leaving the skeleton behind. The burials were of a young man and a young woman, both in their early twenties. They were accompanied by a number of grave goods which would probably have contained food and drink for the journey to the underworld. They included two flagons, one of pottery and the other

*The sarcophagus as it was found in the mausoleum*

J SKEEL

J SKEEL

*Silver spoons found among the grave goods in the mausoleum, and dated to about AD 300. The drop from handle to bowl is characteristic of most Roman spoons*

*Glass gaming counters found on the lid of the young man's coffin*

of bronze, four glass bottles, two glass bowls, two knives and two silver spoons. Placed on the lid of the surviving coffin which contained the young man was a wooden gaming board with a set of 30 glass counters, fifteen white and fifteen red-brown, all decorated with coloured spots. Only one other similar set is known from Roman Britain. A bone inlay, perhaps part of the box to contain the gaming set, was decorated with a mask of Medusa, whose gaze could turn onlookers into stone.

While the evidence allows for the mausoleum to have been robbed and destroyed towards the end of the fourth century when the house church was constructed at the villa, the building was still sufficiently prominent to be known in the late Saxon period when its remains were made use of as part of Lullingstone church.

In addition it is likely that other buildings relating to the working life of the villa as a farm, such as a mill, barns and accommodation for estate workers, remain to be explored both up the slope behind the main house and in the low-lying area between house and river.

*Bone inlay head of Medusa, possibly from the box containing the gaming set*

*Found in the mausoleum, this bronze flagon probably contained drink for the journey to the underworld*

*This rather weathered bust shows a man of about 55. The original is now in the British Museum*

## THE DEVELOPMENT OF THE VILLA

Although there is evidence of first century AD finds from the site, there is no certain evidence for a building at Lullingstone before the late first or early second century AD. By this time the Roman province had been secured as far north as the frontier zone running between the Rivers Solway and Tyne. The site was continuously occupied thereafter until it was destroyed by fire in the fifth century. There were major alterations to the fabric of the building in the second half of the second century and in the later third century, but it is not necessary to assume that a major change of this kind represented a change of owner. Although the presence of the two Greek marble busts may represent evidence of new ownership from the late second or third century, it is possible that the same family with branches elsewhere than in Britain occupied the villa throughout its life. With the exception of the modifications which introduced the Christian rooms in the later fourth century (by which time Christianity had been accepted as the religion of the Roman state), it is not possible to relate any of the changes to the villa to any external influences or events.

*Bronze lion fitting, perhaps an axle-cap, found in the unidentified room and dated to AD 330–350*

## THE EARLY VILLA AD 75–150

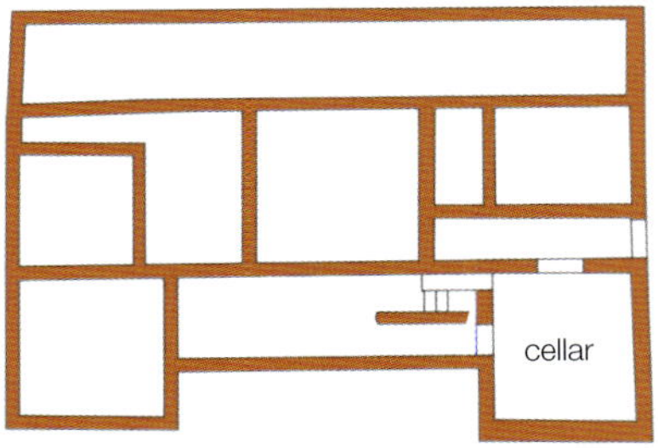


*The compact plan of the early villa has a central block of rooms, fronted by a verandah*

About AD 100 a small villa was built. Much of the evidence of its early history is obscured by later developments. It consisted of a central block of rooms linked by a corridor at the rear and fronted by a verandah. This was flanked by a pair of projecting 'wing' rooms of which the northern one was provided with a deep cellar. This could be approached both from within the house and from outside. The house was built with mortared flint foundations, which may have carried a timber-framed, rather than a masonry superstructure. It is possible that a bath-house was associated with this phase. The circular building was constructed near the villa in the early second century.

## EXPANSION OF THE VILLA AD 150–275

The house was considerably enlarged in the second half of the second century. On the south side, perhaps after 180, a suite of baths was constructed, separated from the main house by a passage. To the north a further suite of rooms and corridors were added with a new projecting room at the north-east corner. A kitchen range was built behind the house on the west side and a well was sunk on the south side of the building.

The deep room was decorated with painted plaster which included date-palm motifs, and a round-headed niche was constructed on the south side in which were depicted representations of three water nymphs. Access to the deep room was now gained only from steps at the north-west corner which in turn could be reached from three further flights of steps from the west, north and east. This aspect of the villa begins to give it a unique quality which sets it apart from others in Britain. The emphasis on the access from the exterior, as well as the new rooms on the north side, suggests the involvement of outsiders in whatever cult was worshipped in the deep room. We cannot be clear about the nature of that cult, although it was associated with water deities, but we can be confident of its existence in the villa from the second half of the second century. It is possible that this cultic activity dates back to the origins of the deep room but there is no clear evidence of its use in the first phase of the villa.

In common with Britain generally there are few finds dating from before the last quarter of the the third century . While the excavator believed that the lack of material indicated abandonment, such few third century coins as there are would support the supposition that the villa was continuously occupied.

At some time in the third century it would seem that the entrance to the cellar was blocked and two marble busts were placed on the steps. The evidence for a cult of ancestors or of household gods derives from two pots placed in pits to receive offerings in front of the steps and thereby assumed to be associated with the busts. These were quite weathered and must

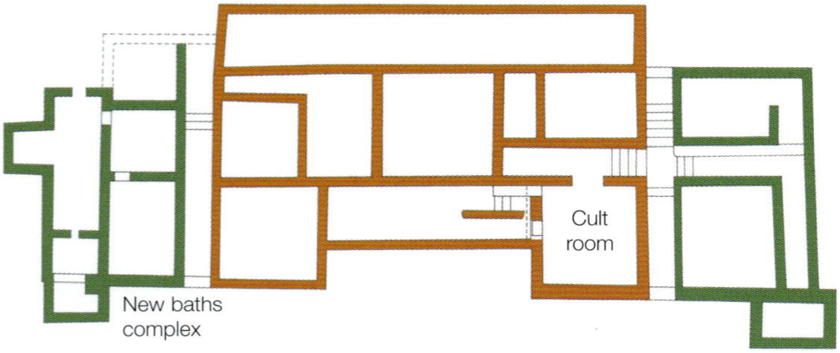


*In this period a new baths complex was added, and to the north further rooms, with formal steps leading to the cult room*

*Wall paintings of a palm tree and purple flower found in the cult room*

*This reconstruction shows the baths after remodelling in the third century. To the right is the plunge pool with a fresco of fishes on the wall. In the centre is the tepid room and on the left the hot water bath. The tank is fed by a leat from the river*

have originally stood elsewhere and outside; when they came to Lullingstone is uncertain. Their position and their association with the buried pots suggests that they might have represented members of the family. Since activity continued to take place in the deep room until the destruction of the villa, it is likely that access to it was via a trap-door from the room above.

## RESHAPING THE VILLA AD 275–350

At the end of the third century the north side of the villa was remodelled by the construction of a row of heated rooms. This was the first time that such rooms had been provided in the villa. Just outside what had served as the original exterior doorway in the west wall was a pit

which had once served to assist drainage. In the early fourth century this had been lined with clay at the base of which were the remains of two millstones, while in the sides were found the fragmentary remains of two ducks. Above these were the well preserved skeletons of two geese with their wings outstretched; one facing north, the other south. There can be little doubt of the ritual nature of this deposit, but considerable uncertainty of its significance to those involved in it.

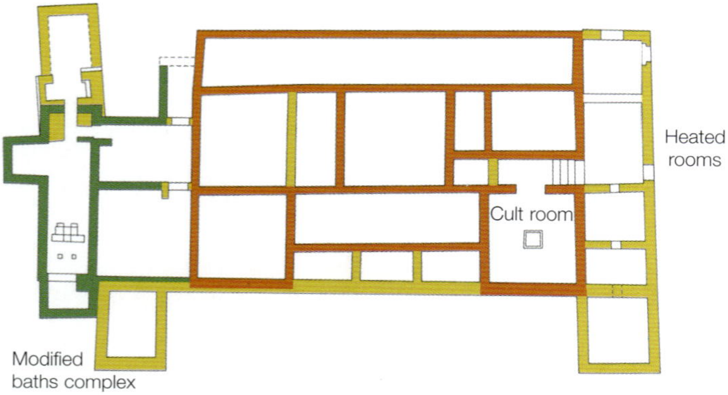

On the south side the baths were altered to include a plunge bath on the east side and to provide an extension to the frigidarium. In the fourth century the east verandah was widened taking it over two earlier foundations, possibly buttressing the original build. Until further work is done outside to establish the location of paths, we cannot be certain whether the principal entrance to the house was located here. The granary and the mausoleum, in which were interred the remains of a young man and a young woman, were built at the beginning of the fourth century. In the mid-fourth century further alterations saw the construction of a large apsed dining room and the laying of a mosaic in the centre of the house.

*With the introduction of the suite of heated rooms, access to the cult room is more limited. The baths have been remodelled and a furnace room and plunge pool added*

*Mosaic detail representing one of the four seasons, autumn, wearing a garland of corn*

*Pieces of Roman tile with dog (left) and kitten (right) footprints pressed into the clay before it was fired*

# ❖ THE MYTHS IN THE MOSAICS ❖

The mosaics depict scenes from two ancient mythological stories. In the semi-circular apse is shown *The Rape of Europa*, in which the supreme Roman god Jupiter, disguised as bull, abducts the princess Europa. She is accompanied by two cupids, one of whom is holding the tail of the bull, perhaps to restrain it. Above Europa's head is an elegaic couplet in Latin:

INVIDASITA[URI]VIDISSET IUNONATATUS
IUSTIUSAEOLIASISSETAD USQUEDOMOS

*(If jealous Juno had seen the swimmings of the bull*
*more justly would she have gone to the hall of Aeolus.)*

This is an allusion to the first book of the Aeneid, by the Latin poet Virgil, where Jupiter's wife Juno, seeing Aeneas at sea with his fleet, visits Aeolus to demand a storm to drown him. Here the reference is ironically transferred to Jupiter's escapade with Europa. Although a similarity has been noted with the style of the Latin poet Ovid, we do not know the author of these lines, which were perhaps specially composed for the Lullingstone floor.

*The abduction of the princess Europa by Jupiter disguised as a bull is shown in the mosaic in the apsed dining room*

*Bellerophon killing the Chimaera* tells how Bellerophon, a prince of Corinth in Greece, was set the task of destroying the fire-breathing she-monster, Chimaera, which had the head of a lion, the body of a goat and a serpent's tail. To help him in his task Bellerophon was advised to catch and tame the winged horse Pegasus. With the aid of a magical bridle Athene helped Bellerophon to do this. Bellerophon is shown in a red cloak and boots, astride Pegasus and piercing the Chimaera's back with his long spear (see page 31). Although rather poorly executed, you can see that the Chimaera has a lion's head, fire coming from her mouth (represented by the red lines), the gaping jaws of a goat projecting from her back, and a serpent's head at the end of her tail.

## THE CHRISTIAN VILLA AD 350–425

Major alterations took place to the northern rooms in the later fourth century. The character of the wall plaster which fell into the cellar beneath indicates that the room above was converted into a Church room. The heated rooms were replaced with an ante-chamber, decorated with painted wall-plaster with Christian symbolism, and a vestibule where the kitchen had stood in the fourth century. Early in the fifth century the house was seriously gutted by fire. The remains of the temple mausoleum were incorporated into Lullingstone church, which is first recorded in 1115. Although the ruins were still visible in the late eighteenth century, nothing survived above ground at the time of the excavation. The gradual erosion of the steep hillside behind the buildings helped to cover and protect the ruins, which is how such complete room plans have survived, unlike other sites.

The continuity of religious activity from at least the second half of the second century (if not from the foundation of the villa) until the early fifth century sets Lullingstone apart from other known villas. The evidence for Christian worship is unequivocal, but there is a fascination in this transitional period at the beginning of the Christian era in seeing the continuity of pagan practice alongside the emergence of the Christian. While Roman Britain provides many parallels for the sort of fine mosaics which decorated the dining and reception rooms of the villa, there is no parallel yet for the painted plaster with Christian symbolism at Lullingstone. Among villas, only at Hinton St Mary in Dorset is there also imagery of a Christian character,

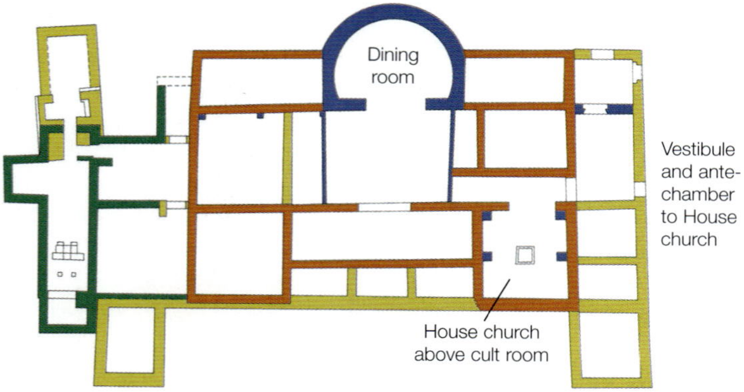


*By the late fourth century the house has an elegant apsed dining room, with a mosaic floor and the house church has been created, although the cult room remained below. The heated rooms were abandoned*

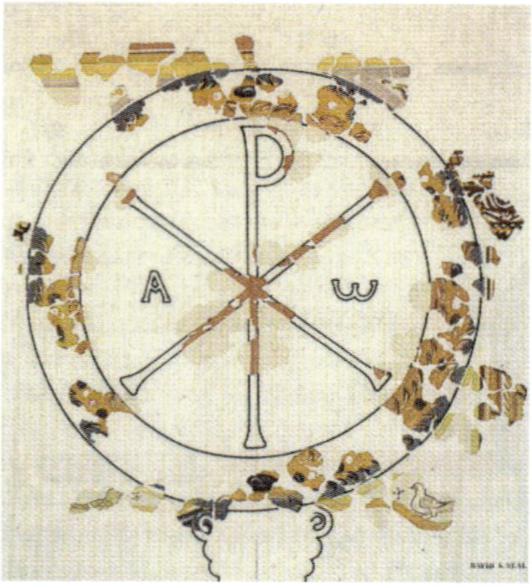


*Painted on the south wall of the ante-chamber to the house church was this Chi-Rho, or Christian monogram, pieced together from fragments*

# ❖ EARLY CHRISTIAN WORSHIP ❖

The writings collected together as *The New Testament* show the rapid spread of Christian communities around the eastern Mediterranean in the first century AD, but there are few sources to tell us when they were first established in Britain. The martyrdoms of St Alban at Verulamium and of Aaron and Julius at Caerleon are likely to have occurred in the third century during one of the many persecutions of the early Christians. These would then strongly imply the presence of Christian communities in Britain by the second century. Evidence that the religion was firmly rooted by the early fourth century is indicated by the attendance of three bishops from York, London and, probably, Lincoln at the Council of Arles in 314, only a year after the Emperor Constantine extended tolerance to Christianity.

*The wall painting of a praying figure from the house church drawn from plaster fragments by David Neal*

Such physical evidence that we have belongs to the fourth century. The remains of churches have been found in towns, as at Colchester and Silchester, in smaller communities such as Icklingham in Suffolk and in the late Roman Saxon Shore fort at Richborough, Kent. The major hoard of Christian silver plate indicates the presence of a church in Water Newton, Cambridgeshire, while, alongside Lullingstone, the villa at Hinton St Mary in Dorset may also have been a place of Christian worship. The survival of a number of lead baptismal tanks decorated with Christian symbols is a further clue to the presence of early churches in the countryside. As far as burial is concerned, the appearance in town and country of inhumation cemeteries with the graves oriented east-west is another likely indicator of Christian communities. The extent of the survival of Christianity in south-east Britain after the end of Roman administration and before St Augustine's mission in Kent in 597 is unclear. However it was Romano-Britons like Saints Patrick and Ninian who spread the gospel to Ireland and Britain beyond Hadrian's Wall during the fifth century.

in this case in the form of a mosaic which is generally regarded as portraying the head of Christ. Religious aspects of the villa are not just represented by the pagan and Christian finds in the deep room. A series of deposits within and near the main house signify a range of beliefs or superstitions throughout the life of the villa; even the well at the south end of the main house produced examples of Stone Pine cones, so often associated with religious ritual. The mosaics are fine works in themselves and without close parallel in Britain. In the representation of Bellerophon slaying the Chimaera, we may see a Christian allegory of the triumph of good over evil.

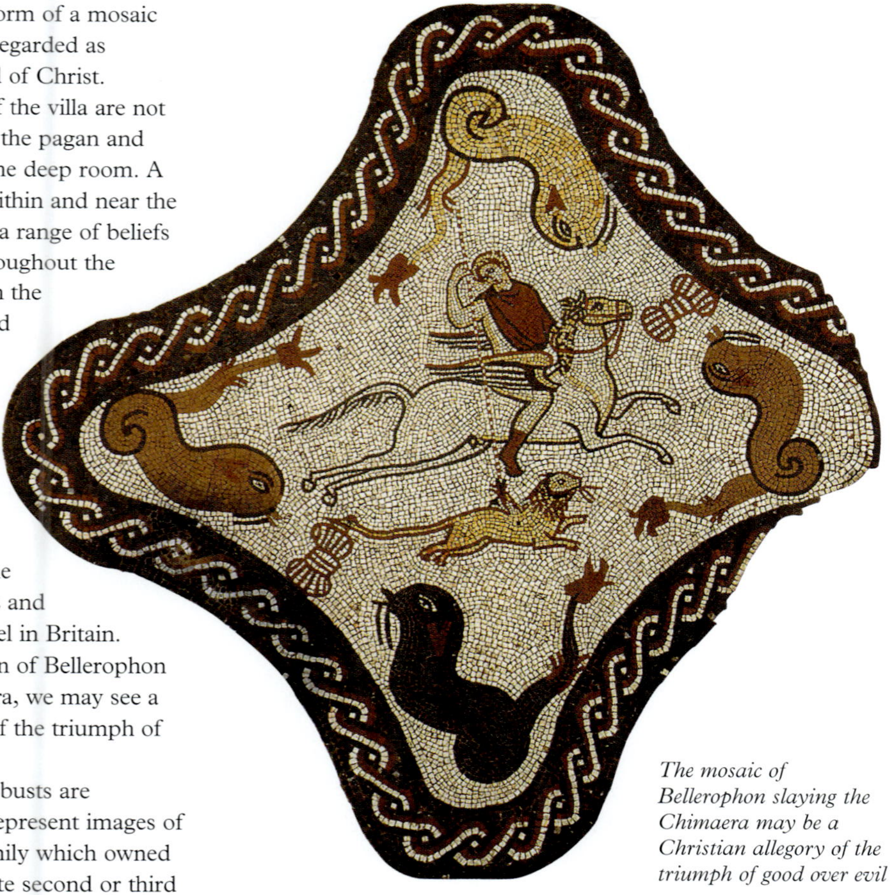

*The mosaic of Bellerophon slaying the Chimaera may be a Christian allegory of the triumph of good over evil*

The two marble busts are intriguing. If they represent images of members of the family which owned the villa from the late second or third century, they indicate a link with the east of the Roman empire. One possibility is that members of the family which first developed the villa enjoyed successful careers in the east, their family or families later returning to their estate in Britain; alternatively the villa changed hands. Without the busts it could well be argued on the basis of the continuing association with religious activity, whether pagan or Christian, that the villa stayed in the same hands throughout its history.

# Lullingstone Roman Villa Plan

## *Further Reading*


G.W.Meates, *The Roman Villa at Lullingstone*, Kent,
—Vol. 1. *The Site*. Tonbridge: Kent Archaeological Society, 1979
—Vol. 2. *The Wall Paintings and Finds*, Maidstone: Kent Archaeological Society, 1987

P. Salway (ed.), *The Roman Era* (The Short Oxford History of the British Isles), Oxford: OUP, 2002.

M. Todd, *Roman Britain* (3rd ed.), London: Fontana, 1999

C. Thomas, *Christianity in Roman Britain to AD 500*, London: Batsford, 1981

D. Perring, *The Roman House in Britain*, London: Routledge, 2002

R. Ling, *Ancient Mosaics*, London: British Museum Press, 1998


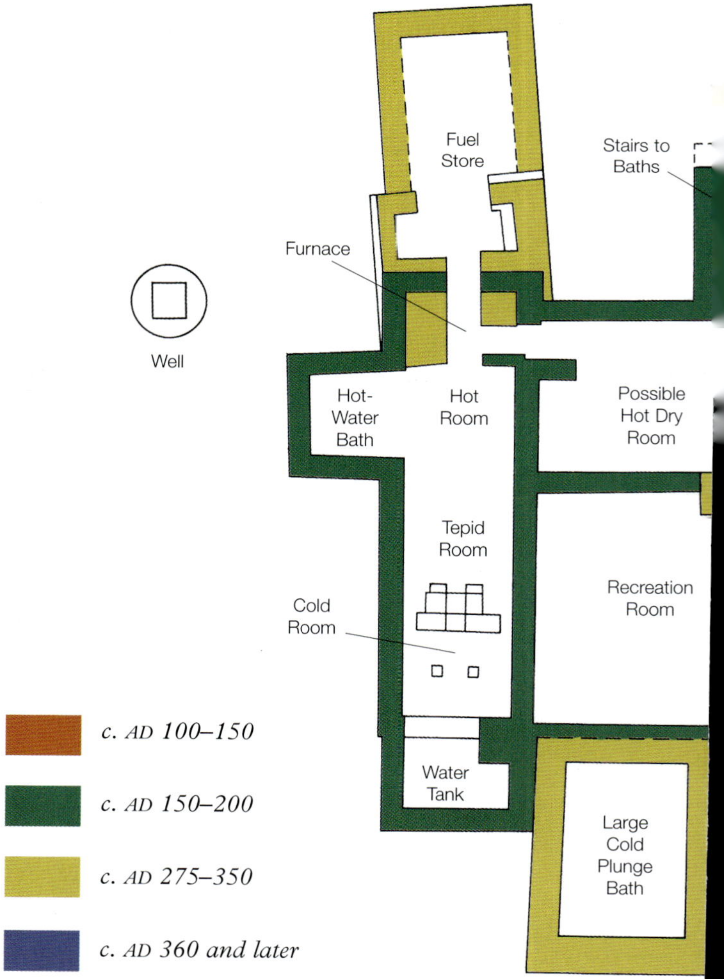